A Long Way Home

A Long Way Home

A Long Way Home

Twelve Years of Words

%

Dwight Yoakam

NEW YORK

Library of Congress Cataloging-in-Publication Data
Yoakam, Dwight
   [Songs. Texts]
   A long way home : twelve years of words / Dwight Yoakam. — 1st ed.
      p. cm.
   ISBN: 0-7868-6514-8
   1. Country Music—Texts.   I. Title
ML54.6.Y63L6   1999
782.421642'0268—dc21   98-49549
                                              CIP
                                             MN

Design by Christine Weathersbee

FIRST EDITION

10 9 8 7 6 5 4 3 2 1

CONTENTS

Gone

Come On Christmas

A Long Way Home

PREFACE

*M*any of the lyrics that follow on these pages began as little more than murmurs, inarticulate, distant whispers. My largest contribution to the revealing of any understanding found in or through them can only be attributed to the slow and arduous process I've gone through in an attempt to learn how not to disturb or interrupt them, while simultaneously hoping to expose their presence through an embrace. At times I have felt, and I continue to feel, that the process has been an embrace of the sense of the isolation that we all contradictorily "share" as a common companion at various times and in varying degrees throughout life.

In trying to learn how to "give over" to the murmurings with each song, I've had to relearn a mental stillness and openness. Because they are so faint, and due to life's constant interference, I've had to learn to remain vigilant in that stillness, so that I can continue to recognize when the footsteps of such murmurs are near and let them seek me out, as if approaching from somewhere behind my physical self, caressing, lifting, and moving me in a variety of directions. With each new song, I continue striving to achieve this passive access to their influence.

Perhaps because time for the world has become so compressed over the last 40 to 50 years, or merely because of the perception of this and of all its accelerated attendant noise, there have been a seemingly ceaseless amount of self-induced interruptions of the connections that I have been able to make with those murmurs. And even when I'm free of the seductive diversions that come with the moments of time and place that, ironically, give the form and shape to emotional expression, I find myself drawn toward seeking out the next intrusion.

In other words, in a feeble attempt to clarify this tangled mess of contradictions, I'm engaged in a continuous struggle to live life in the present tense of each moment, without being so distracted by it that I am incapable of making any pure or meaningful observations about it.

By even attempting this explanation, I find myself falling farther away from being able to give an adequate or truly accurate one. I feel a sense of shame from giving exposure to a triteness and/or confused ridiculousness in the process. But I'm informed that this is a necessity—writing of a preface for the publishing of this book, I mean—even though the very act of trying to explain it would appear to destroy what grace, if any, these lyrics possess. I have taken some small comfort in the contradiction of prefacing emotional expressions, which suffer contamination from and can be brutally undermined by explanation, with this rambling, wrestling brawl of thoughts.

Writing these lyrics has been a journey of discovery for me. Sometimes a slow, tentative, wandering through to it. Other times, an explosive, afterburning launch toward it. But always a gratifying gift of moments of enormous satisfaction for having gained perhaps some small piece of understanding about the things I've seen, touched, heard, or experienced. So, in other words, songwriting is a process of chasing wisps of smoke around a room, and, obviously for me, not an easily or clearly definable one.

What follows is possibly the evidence of love or loss, of hopefulness or regret, of what life may have felt like at a given moment. To read, hear, speak, or sing these words now reminds me of what love, wishfulness, loss, emptiness, and all of life can feel like.

—*Dwight Yoakam*
Los Angeles, California

A Long Way Home

Guitars, Cadillacs, Etc., Etc.
1986

℅

It Won't Hurt

It won't hurt when I fall down from this bar stool
And it won't hurt when I stumble in the street
It won't hurt 'cause this whiskey eases misery
But even whiskey cannot ease your hurting me

Today I had another bout with sorrow
You know this time I almost won
If this bottle would just hold out 'til tomorrow
I know that I'd have sorrow on the run

It won't hurt when I fall down from this bar stool
And it won't hurt when I stumble in the street
It won't hurt 'cause this whiskey eases misery
But even whiskey cannot ease your hurting me

Your memory comes back up with each sunrise
I reach out for the bottle and find it's gone
Yeah, Lord, somewhere every night the whiskey leaves me
To face this cold, cold world on my own

It won't hurt when I fall down from this bar stool
And it won't hurt when I stumble in the street
It won't hurt 'cause this whiskey eases misery
But even whiskey cannot ease your hurting me

I'll Be Gone

I watch as you take off your clothes and slip under the sheets
Then I turn and kick the boots off my feet
I pull you close without a word 'cause there's no need to speak
Girl, beauty like yours is hard to beat

But I'll be gone in the morning, in the morning I'll be gone
'Cause I'm not one for hanging on
So please don't think that you done something wrong
In the morning when you wake and find me gone

Just a look from those fiery eyes can all but erase
The memory of any other's face
And the passion they unleash could cause me to misplace
And lose all track of time without a trace

But I'll be gone in the morning, in the morning I'll be gone
'Cause I'm not one for hanging on
So please don't think that you done something wrong
In the morning when you wake and find me gone

The sun intrudes and throws across the room its golden tracks
Shake the dreams, now it's back to facts
As I turn to leave I know you had what so many lack
Maybe some day that'll bring me back

But I'll be gone in the morning, in the morning I'll be gone
'Cause I'm not one for hanging on
So please don't think that you done something wrong
In the morning when you wake and find me gone

South of Cincinnati

If you ever get south of Cincinnati down where the
　　dogwood trees grow
If you ever get south of the Mason Dixon to the home
　　you left so long ago
If you ever get south of the Ohio River down where
　　Dixieland begins
If you ever get south of Cincinnati I'll be yours again

She pulled the letter from the pages of her Bible
And a rose pressed inside the Book of Luke
For fourteen years she'd write each day but keep it hidden
Refused to even speak his name, but still she wrote

If you ever get south of Cincinnati down where the
　　dogwood trees grow
If you ever get south of the Mason Dixon to the home
　　you left so long ago
If you ever get south of the Ohio River down where
　　Dixieland begins
If you ever get south of Cincinnati I'll be yours again

At a cold gray apartment in Chicago
A cigarette drowns inside a glass of gin
He lies there drunk, but it don't matter drunk or sober
He'll never read the words that pride won't let her send

If you ever get south of Cincinnati down where the
dogwood trees grow
If you ever get south of the Mason Dixon to the home
you left so long ago
If you ever get south of the Ohio River down where
Dixieland begins
If you ever get south of Cincinnati I'll be yours again

Then I'll be yours again

Bury Me

Bury me along the big sandy
Down in those blue, gray mountains
Rest my soul in those hills of coal
Until this old earth does tremble

Now don't you mourn for me when my soul is free
Woman don't you cry
You just bury me along the big sandy
Under a blue Kentucky sky

This old town of sin, it's about to do me in
I don't know how much I can stand
With my knees on the street and my heart at their feet
I'm forced to beg from Satan's hand

So bury me along the big sandy
Down in those blue, gray mountains
Rest my soul in those hills of coal
Until this old earth does tremble

Now don't you mourn for me when my soul is free
Woman don't you cry
You just bury me along the big sandy
Under a blue Kentucky sky

When I came to this land I was strong and I could stand
But now I've somehow gone astray
Yet I still see the truth in the teaching of my youth
And I know that the Lord ain't turned away

So bury me along the big sandy
Down in those blue, gray mountains
Rest my soul in those hills of coal
Until this old earth does tremble

Now don't you mourn for me when my soul is free
Woman don't you cry
You just bury me along the big sandy
Under a blue Kentucky sky

Under a blue Kentucky sky

Guitars, Cadillacs

Girl you taught me how to hurt real bad and cry
   myself to sleep
You showed me how this town can shatter dreams
Another lesson about a naive fool that came to Babylon
And found out that the pie don't taste so sweet

Now it's guitars, Cadillacs and hillbilly music
And lonely, lonely streets that I call home
Yeah those guitars, Cadillacs and hillbilly music
Is the only thing that keeps me hanging on

There ain't no glamour in this tinseled land of lost and
   wasted lives
And painful scars are all that's left of me
But thank you girl for teaching me brand new ways to
   be cruel
And if I can find my mind now, I guess I'll just leave

And it's guitars, Cadillacs and hillbilly music
And lonely, lonely streets that I call home
Yeah those guitars, Cadillacs and hillbilly music
Is the only thing that keeps me hanging on
It's the only thing that keeps me hanging on

It's the only thing that keeps me hanging on

Twenty Years

Hey look yonder, Henry, comes the sheriff
And he's carrying a warrant in his hand
Don't you run, poor old Henry, for he'll shoot you
Not long will you be a free man

Now twenty years you must spend behind steel bars
For a crime that you did not do
Yeah the lie she swore in that district court
Has proved to be the ruin of you

Tried to warn you, Henry, not to cross her
Tried to tell you about her vengeful ways
When you turned and left her for another
She swore, Henry, that she'd make you pay

Now twenty years you must spend behind steel bars
For a crime that you did not do
Yeah the lie she swore in that district court
Has proved to be the ruin of you

Listen well, all you young rounders
Heed the lesson poor old Henry never learned
That even hell with all its fiery power
Hath no fury like a woman's scorn

Now twenty years you must spend behind steel bars
For a crime that you did not do
Yeah the lie she swore in that district court
Has proved to be the ruin of you

Miner's Prayer

When the whistle blows each morning
And I walk down in that cold, dark mine
I say a prayer to my dear Saviour
Please let me see the sunshine one more time

When oh when will it be over
When will I lay these burdens down
And when I die, dear Lord in heaven
Please take my soul from 'neath that cold, dark ground

I still grieve for my poor brother
And I still hear my dear old mother cry
When late that night they came and told her
He'd lost his life down in the Big Shoal Mine

When oh when will it be over
When will I lay these burdens down
And when I die, dear Lord in heaven
Please take my soul from 'neath that cold, dark ground

I have no shame, I feel no sorrow
If on this earth not much I own
I have the love of my sweet children
An old plow mule, a shovel and a hoe

When oh when will it be over
When will I lay these burdens down
And when I die, dear Lord in heaven
Please take my soul from 'neath that cold, dark ground

Yeah when I die, dear Lord in heaven
Please take my soul from 'neath that cold,
    dark ground

*Dedicated to the memory of Luther Tibbs, a Kentucky
coal miner for 40 years and my Grandpa.*

Hillbilly Deluxe
1987

⅍

Little Ways

You've got your little ways to hurt me
You know just how to tear me up
And leave me in small pieces on the ground
You've got your little ways to hurt me
They're not too big but they're real tough
Just one cold look from you can knock me down

To look at you and me, no one would ever know
The pain that I've endured 'cause I won't let it show
My friends would laugh out loud if they only knew
The truth about how I am just your lovesick fool

You've got your little ways to hurt me
You know just how to tear me up
And leave me in small pieces on the ground
You've got your little ways to hurt me
They're not too big but they're real tough
Just one cold look from you can knock me down

The sadness in my eyes should somehow be a clue
But no one here would ever suspect sweet little you
There've been rumors of the truth but I've kept it quiet
'Cause I'm too ashamed to let them know you make me cry

You've got your little ways to hurt me
You know just how to tear me up
And leave me in small pieces on the ground
You've got your little ways to hurt me
They're not too big but they're real tough
Just one cold look from you can knock me down

Johnson's Love

She had left him lost and broken
Like no other had before
And now his heart was just a token
Of the pain it had endured
And his memories were clouded
With all the hurtful things she'd said
Yes, for all intent and purpose
He might just as well been dead

And some people claim
They still hear him call her name
Hey, hey, Maureen,
Swear they hear it just that plain
Deep in the night and
Sometimes right at dawn
See, his body died some years ago
But around here,
Mr. Johnson's love lives on

He seemed far away and distant
With that cold and silent stare
Never moving, never speaking
And just barely breathing air
No one really knew her reason
And who can judge her right or wrong
The only true and solemn fact is,
The man we'd known was all but gone

And some people claim
They still hear him call her name
Hey, hey, Maureen,
Swear they hear it just that plain
Deep in the night and
Sometimes right at dawn
See, his body died some years ago
But around here,
Mr. Johnson's love lives on

Sissy Thompson said she'd seen him
Late that night on Shelby Road
About a mile from there they found him
It seems he'd died out in the snow
I heard the preacher at the service
Say from love he's finally free
But I say love, it knows no season
It haunts the soul eternally

And some people claim
They still hear him call her name
Hey, hey, Maureen,
Swear they hear it just that plain
Deep in the night and
Sometimes right at dawn
See, his body died some years ago
But around here,
Mr. Johnson's love lives on

Please, Please Baby

Please, please baby, baby come back home
'Cause it's so cold and dark here all alone
If you come back I promise I'll be good
If you come home, baby, I'll act like I should

I laughed when you packed your bags
And told me goodbye
I hollered, "I don't need you,"
Aw but honey, that's a lie

Please, please baby, baby come back home
'Cause it's so cold and dark here all alone
If you come back I promise I'll be good
If you come home, baby, I'll act like I should

If you don't come home dear,
I know I'll go insane
Sweetheart, I plead guilty, darlin'
I'll take all the blame

Please, please baby, baby come back home
'Cause it's so cold and dark here all alone
If you come back I promise I'll be good
If you come home, baby, I'll act like I should

Readin,' Rightin,' Rt. 23

They learned readin', rightin', Route 23
To the jobs that lay waiting in those cities' factories
They didn't know that old highway
Could lead them to a world of misery

Have you ever been down Kentucky-way
Say south of Prestonsburg
Have you ever been up in a holler
Or have you ever heard
A mountain man cough his life away
From diggin' that black coal in those dark mines
If you had you might just understand
The reason that they left it all behind

'Cause they'd learned readin', rightin', Route 23
To the jobs that laid waiting in those cities' factories
They learned readin', rightin', roads to the north
To the luxury and comfort a coal miner can't afford
They thought readin', rightin', Route 23
Would take them to the good life that they had never seen
They didn't know that old highway
Could lead them to a world of misery

Have you ever seen 'em put the kids in the car after
    work on Friday night
Pull up in a holler about 2 a.m. and see a light still
    shinin' bright
Those mountain folks sat up that late
Just to hold those little grandkids in their arms
And I'm proud to say that I've been blessed
And touched by their sweet hillbilly charm

But they'd learned readin', rightin', Route 23
To the jobs that laid waiting in those cities' factories
They learned readin,' rightin,' roads to the north
To the luxury and comfort a coal miner can't afford
They thought readin', rightin', Route 23
Would take them to the good life that they had never seen
They didn't know that old highway
Could lead them to a world of misery
They didn't know that old highway
Could lead them to a world of misery

Written for and lovingly dedicated to my mother,
Ruth Ann; to my aunts, Margaret, Mary Helen,
Verdie Kay, and Joy; and to my uncle, Guy Walton.

1,000 Miles

Runway Four, Flight 209
Teardrop falls, we start to climb
This window seat proved a poor choice
It shows the dream that's been destroyed

A little baby starts to cry
Hey, I would too, if not for pride
I owe so much to pride, it's true
It brought an end to me and you

But if I could, I'd turn around
Set my feet back on the ground
'Cause all this plane ride holds for me
Is 1,000 miles of misery

I hear the engines, watch the clouds
The whole damn world looks distant now
But I can't seem to put no space
Between my cold heart and your sweet face

Across the aisle they're holding hands
Revealing brand-new wedding bands
Our sweet gold, it's gone to rust
And now my life has turned to dust

But if I could, I'd turn around
Set my feet back on the ground
'Cause all this plane ride holds for me
Is 1,000 miles of misery

Throughout All Time

I'll still see you walking silently
Through the shadows in my mind

And a vision of your sweet blue eyes
Creeps into my dreamful sleep at night
You still haunt the deepness of my memories
I guess you will throughout all time

Little girl, I still remember
The very dress you wore on that day
It was so soft, a shade of violet, Lord
How it took my breath away

As the sunshine of the morning
Broke across your golden hair
How I wished to hold you tightly
But I was shy and did not dare

I'll still see you walking silently
Through the shadows in my mind

And a vision of your sweet blue eyes
Creeps into my dreamful sleep at night
You still haunt the deepness of my memories
I guess you will throughout all time

Many nights I've sat and wondered
If you might be somebody's wife
But if you're not, I'd long to see you
If just to tell you how I've pined

I've been known to ask of strangers
That I thought might just pass your way
If they would tell you of these feelings
That we might meet again someday

I'll still see you walking silently
Through the shadows in my mind

And a vision of your sweet blue eyes
Creeps into my dreamful sleep at night
You still haunt the deepness of my memories
I guess you will throughout all time

This Drinkin' Will Kill Me

They say this drinkin' will kill me
I don't know, oh Lord, it might be true
If I stop I'll just die from your leavin'
So either way that I go, it's 'cause of you

Death can come from this broken heart
Or it can come from this bottle
So why prolong the agony
Hey, bartender, I think I'll hit the throttle

I don't care how the preacher might preach me
About the evils of being drunk with wine
I don't care how the doctor might warn me
'Cause since you left, it's just a matter of time

Death can come from this broken heart
Or it can come from this bottle
So why prolong the agony
Hey, bartender, I think I'll hit the throttle

I don't care that my friends have all left me
'Cause they swear that I have gone insane
And I don't care anymore about livin'
'Cause without you, just the grave can ease the pain

Death can come from this broken heart
Or it can come from this bottle
So why prolong the agony
Hey, bartender, I think I'll hit the throttle

They say this drinkin' will kill me
I don't know, oh Lord, it might be true
If I stop I'll just die from your leavin'
So either way that I go, it's 'cause of you

Buenas Noches
from a Lonely Room
1988

%

I Got You

I've had to buy back damn near everything I own
From a little man whose name is Saul
And has a lot of money to loan
I drive a beat-up '67 Chevrolet
With a torn-up seat
That pokes a brand-new hole in my back near every day
I got a letter from the folks over at Bell
Just to let me know for my next phone call
I could walk outside and yell
Hey, I know my life seems a mess
But, honey, things to me still look real swell

'Cause I've got you to see me through
Yeah, I've got you to chase my blues
I've got you to ease my pain
Yeah, I've got you, girl, to keep me sane
So let them do what they want to do
'Cause it don't matter long as I've got you

I've got the landlord breathing down my neck for rent
He don't give a damn about my kids or where the
   money was spent
And after all those years of payin' union dues
It sure didn't seem to count for much when we got
   our layoff news

I got a note from the man over at the bank
Said the next 10 gallons of gas I buy won't be
    going in my tank
Hey, I know I might seem near dead
But honey, I think I might just get well

'Cause I've got you to see me through
Yeah, I've got you to chase my blues
I've got you to ease my pain
Honey, I've got you, girl, to keep me sane
So let them do what they want to do
'Cause it don't matter long as I've got you

Yeah, let them go right ahead and sue
'Cause it don't matter long as I've got you

One More Name

My friends tried to tell me you were steppin' around
But I wouldn't hear it, I shut them all down
But now I'm a thinkin' you've made a fool out of me
'Cause the words that are slippin' spell grief and misery

One more name, one more name you call out in your sleep
One more name and I'll know it's not a lie
One more name, one more name that from your lips does creep
One more name and our love will surely die

Haunted and tortured by the rumors about you
Listening in silence to whispers of truth
Deceived by the soft kiss you forge every day
While each night those same lips give your secret away

One more name, one more name you call out in your sleep
One more name and I'll know it's not a lie
One more name, one more name that from your lips does creep
One more name and our love will surely die

One more name, one more name you call out in your sleep
One more name and I'll know it's not a lie
One more name, one more name that from your lips does creep
One more name and our love will surely die

What I Don't Know

What I don't know might not hurt me
If I stay dumb and no one tells
But if I find out that you've been cheatin'
What I don't know might get you killed

Death row in prison don't look half as bad
As a life filled with heartache over you
So if you're a playin' those dirty little games
You better pray that I don't find out the truth

'Cause what I don't know might not hurt me
If I stay dumb and no one tells
But if I find out that you've been cheatin'
What I don't know might get you killed

Smith and Wesson juries hold a real mean, nasty court
And the verdict that they pass is never slow
So keep on a wearin' that little poker face
'Cause soon enough your cards will have to show

And what I don't know might not hurt me
If I stay dumb and no one tells
But if I find out that you've been cheatin'
What I don't know might get you killed

Buenas Noches from a Lonely Room

(She Wore Red Dresses)

She wore red dresses with her black shining hair
She had my baby and caused me to care
Then coldly she left me to suffer and cry
She wore red dresses and told such sweet lies

I never knew him but he took her away
And on my knees like a madman for vengeance I prayed
While the pain and the anger destroyed my weak mind
She wore red dresses and left the wounded behind

I searched till I found them, then I cursed at the sight
Of their sleeping shadows in the cold neon light
In the dark morning silence I placed the gun to her head
She wore red dresses, but now she lay dead

I Sang Dixie

I sang Dixie as he died
The people just walked on by as I cried
The bottle had robbed him of all his rebel pride
So I sang Dixie as he died

He said, Way down yonder in the land of cotton
Old times there ain't near as rotten as they are
On this damned old L.A. street
Then he drew a dying breath
And laid his head against my chest
Please, Lord, take his soul back home to Dixie

I sang Dixie as he died
The people just walked on by as I cried
The bottle had robbed him of all his rebel pride
So I sang Dixie as he died

He said, Listen to me son, while you still can
Run back home to that Southern land
Don't you see what life here has done to me?
Then he closed those old blue eyes
And fell limp against my side
No more pain, now he's safe back home in Dixie

I sang Dixie as he died
The people just walked on by as I cried
The bottle had robbed him of all his rebel pride
So I sang Dixie as he died

I sang Dixie as he died

Floyd County

It's a sad day in Floyd County, Mr. Jones
Yeah, the grief is strong for the man that's gone
And at the grave his woman cries and she moans
'Cause it's a sad day in Floyd County, Mr. Jones

The six children he raised are all weepin'
For this soft-spoken mountain man
Who fed them with the money he earned in those black mines
And the food he could raise with his hands

It's a sad day in Floyd County, Mr. Jones
Yeah, the grief is strong for the man that's gone
And at the grave his woman cries and she moans
'Cause it's a sad day in Floyd County, Mr. Jones

Though the world knew nothing of his wisdom
Or the honest and simple things he did
There's some folks cryin' on this hillside today
That know about the humble way he lived

It's a sad day in Floyd County, Mr. Jones
Yeah, the grief is strong for the man that's gone
And at the grave his woman cries and she moans
'Cause it's a sad day in Floyd County, Mr. Jones

Now this house in the holler stands empty
Though his presence in my memory is plain
You know I'd swear that I just saw him
A-walkin' up that hill
I guess this place just won't never be the same

It's a sad day in Floyd County, Mr. Jones
Yeah, the grief is strong for the man that's gone
And at the grave his woman cries and she moans
'Cause it's a sad day in Floyd County, Mr. Jones

Hold On to God

Hold on, hold on, hold on to God
And not the ways of the world
Hold on, hold on and put your trust
In His ever lasting Word

Hold on, hold on, hold on to God
In this life's storm-tossed sea
Cling to Jesus, His lifeline
It will salvation bring

Satan shall lead down a pathway of sin
Away from your heavenly home
With many great wonders, many great signs
Deceiving all but the strong

Hold on, hold on, hold on to God
And not the ways of the world
Hold on, hold on and put your trust
In His ever lasting Word

Hold on, hold on, hold on to God
In this life's storm-tossed sea
Cling to Jesus, His lifeline
It will salvation bring

Be not misled by miraculous deeds
Performed in the name of the Lamb
For He shall return as a thief in the night
To claim his own once again

Hold on, hold on, hold on to God
And not the ways of the world
Hold on, hold on and put your trust
In His ever lasting Word

Written and performed for my mother,
Ruth Ann, without whose love and support
I would not have survived at three months
or thirty years of age. Your hands will
always guide my heart.

If There Was a Way
1990

%

The Distance Between You and Me

Take a rock, tie a rope
Throw it down in the sea
Let it fall to the bottom
Nobody knows how deep
Stare real hard through the water
And you might just perceive
The distance between you and me
The distance between you and me

Take a map of the world
And measure with your hand
All of the miles
Across all of the land
Write it down, add it up
And you might understand
About the distance between you and me
The distance between you and me

I lie awake and hear you breathing
Only inches from me in this bed
Not much space but it's all that we needed
To live alone now that our love is dead

Climb the earth's tallest mountain
To where it reaches the sky
Take a gun, fire a bullet
Straight up out of sight
Where it stops in the heavens
Well, that ain't half as high
As the distance between you and me

The distance between you and me

The Heart That You Own

I pay rent on a run-down place
There ain't no view but there's lots of space
In my heart
The heart that you own
I pay the rent
Pay it right on time
Baby, I pay you every single dime
For my heart
The heart that you own

Used to be I could love here for free
Way back before you bought the property
Now I pay daily on what once was mine
Lord, I probably owe you
For the tears that I cry

'Cause I pay rent on a run-down place
There ain't no view but there's lots of space
In my heart
The heart that you own

I struggle each night to find a new way
To pay what I owe
Just so I can stay
I ain't overdue
So you can't throw me out
I've loved here for years
Don't know where I'd go now

'Cause I pay rent on a run-down place
There ain't no view but there's lots of space
In my heart
The heart that you own

Takes a Lot to Rock You

Takes a lot to rock you baby
It takes a lot to make you smile
It takes a lot to rock you baby
You make me crawl the extra mile

So much for wishful thinkin'
So much for beginner's luck
It takes a lot to rock you baby
When it come to love you're double-tough

Takes a lot to rock you baby
It takes a lot to make you smile
It takes a lot to rock you baby
You make me crawl the extra mile

Little things that used to please you
Are all the things that I do wrong
It takes a lot to rock you baby
Tried my damnedest all night long

My baby drives a big Rolls Royce
'Cause my baby says she got no choice
My baby wear big ol' diamond rings
'Cause my baby says she need them things

Takes a lot to rock you baby
It takes a lot to make you smile
It takes a lot to rock you baby
You make me crawl the extra mile

Nothing's Changed Here

I hear you walking across the floor
I think that I'm dreaming
'Til I hear you shut the door
I wake up crying and calling your name
Nothing's changed here without you
I start every day the same

The same old sun comes up to shine
On this old bed at the same old time
I tell myself the same old lie
I've got you off my mind

I feel your body lyin' next to mine
I reach out in the darkness
But you're not there for me to find
There's only sorrow followed by pain
Nothing's changed here without you
I start every day the same

I see your sweet lips softly kiss me goodbye
I taste the salt of my teardrops
As they fall down from my eyes
I take a deep breath
But it's only in vain
'Cause nothing's changed here without you
I start every day the same

I start every day the same

Sad, Sad Music

There should be music
Sad, sad music
But this silence that you left
Is all I have

I must have missed a couple days
Or just forgotten
What went wrong or where it all
Fell apart
And I know you must have told me
You were leavin'
It just never crossed my mind
You'd take my heart

There should be music
Sad, sad music
The kind the movies have
When love like ours goes bad
There should be music
Sad, sad music
But this silence that you left
Is all I have

I'd swear that I woke up with you
This morning
But I can see that it's been days
Since you were here
And every night it still hits home
Without a warning
As my world becomes a flood of
Scalding tears

There should be music
Sad, sad music
As you walk away without
Looking back
There should be music
Sad, sad music
But this silence that you left
Is all I have

There should be music

Since I Started Drinkin' Again

Since I started drinkin' again
Since I started drinkin' again
I ain't shed one lousy tear over you
Since I started drinkin' again

I know that the neighbors are all a-talkin'
They swear that I have lost my mind
Ah but they do not know
That I've just gained control
Of all the heartache that you left behind

Since I started drinkin' again
Since I started drinkin' again
I ain't shed one lousy tear over you
Since I started drinkin' again

Well, I know that the boss is gonna fire me
When I stumble in late to work again
But surprise will replace that old scowl on his face
When he sees that I do not give a damn

Since I started drinkin' again
Since I started drinkin' again
I ain't shed one lousy tear over you
Since I started drinkin' again

If There Was a Way

I was just standing
Alone in this room
Surrounded by memories
We stopped making too soon
I was just standing
I was just standing
Alone in this room
Alone in this room

I was just thinking
All to myself
How I still want you
And nobody else
I was just thinking
I was just thinking
All to myself
All to myself

In this darkness I move slowly
Always struggling to be free
But I still hear your voice
And everywhere I see the choice
That's made such a fool of me

I was just wondering
If there was a way
To bring you back to me
Maybe things I could say
I was just wondering

I was just wondering
If there was a way

It Only Hurts When I Cry

The only time I feel the pain
Is in the sunshine or the rain
And I don't feel no hurt at all
Unless you count when teardrops fall
I tell the truth 'cept when I lie
And it only hurts me when I cry

You couldn't tell it by this smile
But my recovery took a while
I worked for days and nights on end
Just to walk and talk again
You can't believe the time it takes
To heal a heart once it breaks

The only time I feel the pain
Is in the sunshine or the rain
And I don't feel no hurt at all
Unless you count when teardrops fall
I tell the truth 'cept when I lie
And it only hurts me when I cry

Oh maybe every now and then
I have a small heartache again
You wouldn't know to look at me
There's tiny scars that you can't see
It was a struggle to survive
I'm probably lucky I'm alive

The only time I feel the pain
Is in the sunshine or the rain
And I don't feel no hurt at all
Unless you count when teardrops fall
I tell the truth 'cept when I lie
And it only hurts me when I cry

I tell the truth 'cept when I lie
And it only hurts me when I cry

You're the One

You're the one
You're the one
That made me cry
You're the one
That laughed at me
Then said goodbye
You're the one
You're the one
That made me blue
So how's it feel
Now that you're the one
It's happenin' to

Now you're back calling me with open arms
What happened to the one you met with all that charm
You say he's gone
And you're alone
Well that's a shame
But if you think real hard
I know you'll see
Just who's to blame

You're the one
You're the one
That made me cry
You're the one
That laughed at me
Then said goodbye
You're the one
You're the one
That made me blue
So how's it feel
Now that you're the one
It's happenin' to

You're begging me to think about the love we shared
Yet it seems to me not too long ago you didn't care
The love you left
No longer lives
Within my heart
The game you played
So recklessly
Tore it all apart

You're the one
You're the one
That made me cry
You're the one
That laughed at me
Then said goodbye
You're the one
You're the one
That made me blue
So how's it feel
Now that you're the one
It's happenin' to

Oh tell me how's it feel now that you're the one
How's it feel to be the one
How's it feel now that you're the one it's happened to

Dangerous Man

He's a dangerous man
He's got blood in his plans
Better watch out where you stand
'Cause he's a dangerous man
He'll make you believe that he's your friend
But don't forget it's just pretend
And he's a dangerous man

He'll tell you the right things
About all the wrong people
He'll smile and he'll say Hey you and me
We think just the same
You better make sure that you read
All the rules first
'Cause he runs a crooked game

He's a dangerous man
He's got blood in his plans
Better watch out where you stand
'Cause he's a dangerous man
He'll make you believe that he's your friend
But don't forget it's just pretend
And he's a dangerous man

His words are all vain
And his promise is empty
His message is loud
But it ain't meant to be clear
He hides all the clues
That have left his hands stained and dirty
And he'll wash them with your tears

'Cause he's a dangerous man
He's got blood in his plans
Better watch out where you stand
'Cause he's a dangerous man
He'll make you believe that he's your friend

But don't forget it's just pretend
And he's a dangerous man

La Croix D'Amour
1992

Doin' What I Did

Hey, when C.C. Rider
Was just a snot-nosed kid
I was already known
For doin' what I did

The women all screamed
As I walked by
My daddy would cuss me
And my momma'd start to cry

'Cause I was known
For doin' what I did
My reputation was strong
For doin' what I did

There ain't no way
They could ever kept it hid
'Cause I was just too well known
For doin' what I did

My momma called the preacher
Called up everyone she knew
But all of their praying
Did no good for you-know-who

When ol' Cassanova
Was a lovesick punk
I'd already broke so many hearts
I could have started me a dump

'Cause I was known
For doin' what I did

My reputation was strong
For doin' what I did

There ain't no way
They could ever kept it hid
'Cause I was just too well known
For doin' what I did

The older boys were teasin'
On my first day of school
'Til a fine lady teacher
Let me break all her rules

The press heard about it
Tried to put me in the news
But the women had no comment
For fear what they'd lose

'Cause I was known
For doin' what I did
My reputation was strong
For doin' what I did

And there ain't no way
They could ever kept it hid
'Cause I was just too well known
For doin' what I did

Oh, it was like I was grown
Yeah, I was born
Man, I stood alone

Yeah, baby I was strong
At doin' what I did

This Time
1993

❧

The Pocket of a Clown

Inside the pocket of a clown
Is a sad place to hang around
Just watching smiles turn into frowns
Inside the pocket of a clown

Inside the heartache of a fool
You'll learn things they don't teach in school
And lessons there can be real cruel
Inside the heartache of a fool

Hollow lies
Make a thin disguise
As little drops of truth
Fall from your eyes

Inside a memory from the past
Lives every love that didn't last
And sweet dreams can start to fade real fast
Inside a memory from the past

A Thousand Miles from Nowhere

I'm a thousand miles from nowhere
Time don't matter to me
'Cause I'm a thousand miles from nowhere
And there's no place I want to be

I got heartaches in my pocket
I got echoes in my head
And all that I keep hearing
Are the cruel, cruel things that you said

I'm a thousand miles from nowhere
Time don't matter to me
'Cause I'm a thousand miles from nowhere
And there's no place I want to be

I got bruises on my memory
I got tear stains on my hands
And in the mirror there's a vision
Of what used to be a man

I'm a thousand miles from nowhere
Time don't matter to me
'Cause I'm a thousand miles from nowhere
And there's no place I want to be

Home for Sale

Home for sale
That's much too large
Too many rooms
Big ol' empty yard
Far more space
Than the owner needs
Price includes
All memories

Home for sale
Restored like new
Just a place
Two lives outgrew
A change in heart
Forces move away
Would like to keep
But just can't stay

Listen close and you might hear the sound
Of what you think is rainfall leaking down
The roof is fine
Set aside your fears
It's just a few remaining tears

Home for sale
Not all that old
A family's dream
Stands dark and cold
Scenic views
That go for free
Of all the love
That used to be

Home for sale
That's much too large

This Time

This time
Is the last time
That I'll ever call her name
This time
Is the last time
That I'll ever play her game
And this time
Is the last time
That I'll endure this pain
'Cause this time
Is the last time
She'll ever hurt me again

I tell myself each morning
That we're through
But every night I see
That it's not true
I run out
And track her down
Just so I can hang around
And cry

But this time
Is the last time
That I'll ever call her name
This time
Is the last time
That I'll ever play her game

And this time
Is the last time
That I'll endure this pain
'Cause this time
Is the last time
She'll ever hurt me again

Come on heart let's make believe we're fine
We'll both agree the pain's just in our mind
I'll close my eyes and try not to hear
The things I'll say when she appears
To haunt me

'Cause this time
Is the last time
That I'll ever call her name
This time
Is the last time
That I'll ever play her game
And this time
Is the last time
That I'll endure this pain
'Cause this time
Is the last time
She'll ever hurt me again

Two Doors Down

Two doors down there's a jukebox
That plays all night long
Real sad songs
All about me and you
Two doors down there's a barmaid
That serves 'em real strong
Here lately
That's how I make it through
Two doors down there's a heartache
That once was my friend
Two doors down there's a memory
That won't ever end

Two doors down there's a barstool
That knows me by name
And we sit there together
And wait for you
Two doors down there's a bottle
Where I take out my shame
And hold it up
For the whole world to view
Two doors down there's a pay phone
But no calls come in
Two doors down there's a memory
That won't ever end

From the hotel to the barroom
Is just a stumble and a fall
And sometimes when it gets bad
I've been known to crawl
Freedom from sorrow
Is just two doors away
I'll escape for a short time
But I know I can't stay

Two doors down is where they'll find me
When you're finally through
Taking what's left of my life
Two doors down is where they'll leave me
When payment comes due
For the hours I've spent there each night
Two doors down I'll be forgotten
But until then
Two doors down there's a memory
That won't ever end

King of Fools

As you look into my eyes
And tell those empty lies
I'll pretend they're true
'Cause that's what I do

As you sit and hold my hand
And smile at other men
I'll pretend I'm blind
'Cause I'm just that kind

I'm the king of fools
And I'll always reign
Over loneliness and pain
The king of fools wears his crown
Wherever misery can be found

As you walk away with him
And I lose in love again
I'll pretend to see
That you're still with me
But I'll be there all alone
Like a king upon a throne
'Cause I'm the king of fools

I'm the king of fools

Fast as You

Maybe someday I'll be strong
Maybe it won't be long
I'll be the one who's tough
You'll be the one who's got it rough
It won't be long and
Maybe I'll be real strong

Maybe I'll do things right
Maybe I'll start tonight
You'll learn to cry like me
Baby let's just wait and see
Maybe I'll start tonight
And do things right

You'll control me
And oh so boldly
Rule me 'til I'm free
'Til the pain that shakes me
Finally makes me
Get up off of my knees

Maybe I'll be as fast as you
Maybe I'll break hearts too
I think that you'll slow down
When your turn to hurt comes around
Maybe I'll break hearts
And be as fast as you

You'll control me
And oh so boldly
Rule me 'til I'm free
'Til the pain that shakes me
Finally makes me
Get up off of my knees

Maybe I'll be as fast as you
Maybe I'll break hearts too
I think that you'll slow down
When your turn to hurt comes around
Maybe I'll break hearts
And be as fast as you

Try Not to Look So Pretty

Try not to look so pretty
The next time that we meet
Please don't look so pretty
And I won't act so weak
Please don't look so pretty
You're lovely but it's just cruel
Try not to look so pretty
And I'll try not to be your fool

You walk in and steal my mind
But who gave you the right
To treat me like some useless thought
You throw away each night

Please don't look so pretty
You're lovely but it's just cruel
Try not to look so pretty
And I'll try not to be your fool

You make it hard on me
But I'll try to pretend
That you're just a lovesick dream
That always has to end

Please don't look so pretty
You're lovely but it's just cruel
Try not to look so pretty
And I'll try not to be your fool

Wild Ride

I walked in
There sat Slim
Cleaning up his memory with some sapphire gin
Mr. Paine grabbed my arm
Pulled me aside
And said, Kid, are you ready for the wild ride?

I looked up
There she stood
I said, If you didn't look so great
I'd say you look good
She took her hand
Ran it up my thigh
And said, Cowboy, you ready for the wild ride?

Come on now, Junior, take the wild ride
See, can you make it on the wild ride
Don't try no shakin' on the wild ride
'Cause things start breakin' on the wild ride

Layin' on the highway
I saw my mind
In tiny little pieces thrown from side to side
My heart was shattered along with my pride
Guess you can't keep 'em on the wild ride

Come on now, Junior, take the wild ride
See, can you make it on the wild ride
Don't try no shakin' on the wild ride
'Cause things start breakin' on the wild ride

I was crawlin' 'cross the floor
I was trying to leave
When I felt something tuggin' what was left of my sleeve
I heard a little voice with a gold-plated vibe
Say I bought a ticket for the wild ride

Come on, Junior, take the wild ride
See, can we make it on the wild ride
Let's try to shake it on the wild ride
We might just break it on the wild ride

Come on, come on
Take me on the wild ride
See, can you make me on the wild ride
Come on an' shake me on the wild ride
You might just break me on the wild ride

Lonesome Roads

Where did I go wrong
You know I've never had a clue
I must have just been born no good
'Cause bad's the best that I can do

Was it just my fate in life
To end up here this way
Lost and all alone
One more black lamb
That's gone astray

Lonesome roads are the only kind I ever travel
Empty rooms are the only place I ever stay
I'm just a face out in the crowd that looks like trouble
Poor ol' worthless me is the only friend I ever made

Lonesome roads are the only kind I ever travel
Empty rooms are the only place I ever stay
I'm just a face out in the crowd that looks like trouble
Poor ol' worthless me is the only friend I ever made

Gone
1995

⁂

Sorry You Asked?

You'll be sorry you asked me the reason
That she's not here with me tonight
And I know you were probably just acting polite
But you'll be sorry you ever asked why

We started having problems in August last year
So things had been kinda rough for quite awhile
And you know how you think it'll work itself out
Well, mister, that thought's wrong by a long, long mile

You'll be sorry you asked me the reason
That she's not here with me tonight
And I know you were probably just acting polite
But you'll be sorry you ever asked why

I mighta, shoulda seen that we were drifting apart
But I was in what I guess you'd call denial
And I always heard they say that you're the last one to know
Well, buddy, I was last by a long, long while

You'll be sorry you asked me the reason
That she's not here with me tonight
And I know you were probably just acting polite
But you'll be sorry you ever asked why

Okay, we both have the tendency to overreact
So I can't really tell you who's at fault
But there were certain third parties, well her sister for one
Who helped bring our reconciling to a drop-dead halt

Now aren't you sorry you asked me the reason
That she's not here with me tonight
And I know you were probably just acting polite
But I'm sure sorry you ever asked why

Aren't you sorry you ever asked why
I'm sure sorry you ever asked why

Did I tell you how she tried to have me locked out
  of the house
I had to go hire a lawyer and all
But I know that it was mostly her family's idea
I could hear 'em tell her what to say every time I'd call

Near You

Everywhere you go each day
I will be near you
Oh and dear you
Don't even have to say much
For me to hear you
Because it's clear you
Have a very simple way
To keep me near you

Oh yeah dear
Through the power of love
Through the power of love

Every morning, night and noon
I will be near you
Oh and dear you
Won't even have to do much
For me to feel you
Are sincere you
Like a magnet pull so strong
It keeps me near you

Oh yeah dear
Through the power of love
Through the power of love

I could try to just lie
And tell people I'm free
Like a wave tellin' sand
It won't go back to the sea
But what I say doesn't do no good
Like I ever thought it would

Everywhere you go each day
I will be near you
Oh and dear you
Don't even have to say much
For me to hear you
Because it's clear you
Have a very simple way
To keep me near you

Oh yeah dear
Through the power of love
Through the power of love

The power of love

Don't Be Sad

Don't be sad 'cause you got what you wanted
You should be glad to know that I'm finally gone
Don't feel bad or be disappointed
'Cause you got what you wanted all along

Wasn't it you who said a
Blinded fool could see the
Clear plain truth about how
Deeply cruel it is to
Live a lie here with each other
And mourn a life that won't recover
As I recall those were the very words I heard you use

Don't be sad 'cause you got what you wanted
You should be glad to know that I'm finally gone
Don't feel bad or be disappointed
'Cause you got what you wanted all along

Wasn't it me who asked so
Stupidly if there were
Things that I could maybe
Do or try to somehow
Hold what fell apart together
But you just coldly told me never
To even entertain the thought that our love would survive

Don't be sad 'cause you got what you wanted
You should be glad to know that I'm finally gone
Don't feel bad or be disappointed
'Cause you got what you wanted all along

Gone (That'll Be Me)

That'll be me you'll see
Walking away
That'll be me you'll see
For the last time today
That'll be me you'll see
For not very long
'Cause that'll be me
You'll see
That'll be gone

Remember how you warned me
'Bout all your leavin' plans
Well I know this might seem unexpected
So prepare yourself
The best you can

That'll be me you'll see
Walking away
That'll be me you'll see
For the last time today
That'll be me you'll see
For not very long
'Cause that'll be me
You'll see
That'll be gone

Think back on when you threatened
And never left no doubt
Although this could be kinda sudden
I'm sure you can
Figure it all out

That'll be me you'll see
Walking away
That'll be me you'll see
For the last time today
That'll be me you'll see
For not very long
'Cause that'll be me
You'll see
That'll be gone

Nothing

I couldn't change your heart
I couldn't change your mind
So I just had to learn to live with
This empty life you left behind

You didn't try to hear
You didn't try to see
You just stared right through the teardrops
Like there was nothing left of me

Nothing but sorrow, nothing but pain
Nothing but memories that whisper your name
Nothing but sadness, nothing but fear
Nothing but silence is heard around here

Bridges were burned
Lessons were learned
Promises made that were broken
Tender lies softly spoken

Nothing but sorrow, nothing but pain
Nothing but memories that whisper your name
Nothing but sadness, nothing but fear
Nothing but silence is heard around here

Never Hold You

I've seen 'em watch you and
Make plans what they'll do when
Someday you are no longer mine

I've heard 'em carry on about
How when I'm finally gone they're
Gonna treat you oh so fine

But I could have told them that
They'd never hold you if they tried

I could have told them
You bend and fold men who
Thought they would have you as a prize
I could have told them
Those foolish soul'd men that
They'd never hold you if they tried

I've been made real aware of
Pleasure that they'll share with
You soon as I slip your mind

I've listened to 'em boast how
I'll just be a ghost once
They start takin' up your time

But I could have told them that
They'd never hold you if they tried

This Much I Know

This much I know
She'll never come back to me
This much I know
She meant what she said
This much I know
It's taught me all about misery
I just learn kinda slow
This much I know

This much I feel
I should have reached out to her
This much I feel
I tried it too late
This much I feel
How empty the world can be
And so painfully real
This much I feel

I've had second thoughts about
Every reason
We let love slip away
From our lives
And there's no place left to look
That I don't see some
Small reminder
Of all the chances
I just let go by

This much I need
To wake up once and find she's not gone
This much I need
But I'll never have
This much I need
Words to speak without missing her
Or just some new way to breathe
This much I need

Baby Why Not

Oh baby why not
Just take one more chance
And risk all we got
On this luckless romance
If someone asks why
We'll say we forgot
And went kinda crazy
Oh baby why not

If love needs a fool
For it to survive
It sure looks to me
Like we both qualify
And a pair of fools
Will always beat one
So let's play the cards
And get this deal done

Oh baby why not
Bet big on the bliss
And laugh in the face
Of what all odds insist
If someone asks why
We'll say we forgot
And both lost our minds
Oh baby why not

Oh baby please
You and I
Are exactly what we need
So let's throw away all care
Move out on the edge somewhere
Find a place and just swing there in the breeze

Oh baby why not
Just take one more chance
And risk all we got
On this luckless romance
If someone asks why
We'll say we forgot
And threw our lives away
Oh baby why not

And went kinda crazy
Oh baby why not

And both lost our minds
Oh baby why not

One More Night

One more night and I know
That I'll be over you
One more night and I know
That the worst is through
And if I can make this heart
Just believe it too
Then one more night and I know
That I'll be over you

One more night and I know
That I'll forget your voice
One more night and I know
That I can make that choice
And ignore the awful sounds
That come when love's destroyed
One more night and I know
That I'll forget your voice

I'll escape it
If I learn to take it
And just survive two or three
Of the next million thoughts
That I have about you and me

One more night and I know

Heart of Stone

This heart of stone sure is missing you
Sure is wishing you were back where love belongs
This heart of stone has not forgotten you
But broke while trying to pretend that it was strong

Memories have made its will grow tired and weak
Silently it turned from being bold to meek
'Til finally it gave in to a sad defeat
Aching more and more with every fragile beat

This heart of stone sure is missing you
Sure is wishing you were back where love belongs
This heart of stone has not forgotten you
But broke while trying to pretend that it was strong

Loneliness has slowly stripped it of its pride
Leaving just an empty well here behind
Without a hope of any way it could survive
Stranded there alone and simply left to die

This heart of stone sure is missing you
Sure is wishing you were back where love belongs
This heart of stone has not forgotten you
But broke while trying to pretend that it was strong

Come On Christmas
1997

§

Come On Christmas

Come on Christmas
Please take me away
Keep me hidden safe
'Til January's second day
Come on Christmas
Come on Noel

I'll wrap myself up in the cheer
That's so abundant
This time of year
Come on Christmas
Come on Noel

Even though it's just September
I can forget to remember
All the empty nights
Still in my way

Come on Christmas
Embrace me with some joy
'Til the last few lonely moments
Of this year have been destroyed
Come on Christmas
Come on Noel

I'll just let visions of the season
Blind these worn-out sights
Still in my mind
Come on Christmas
Come on Noel

Come on Christmas

Santa Can't Stay

Cold tears fall from his eyes
As he turns into the night and walks away
Lucille runs outside
Just to see if there might be a sleigh
Little Bobby stares down
At the plate where cookies still lay
And tries to understand
Why Momma said Santa can't stay

Momma said Santa can't stay
Said she told him that twice yesterday
Then a car just like Dad's
Pulled out and drove away
After Mom said Santa couldn't stay

They both heard him coming
Saw Mom run down the hall and holler, Wait
Doug you're drunk don't come inside
I'm not joking I've had all this I can take
He threw a present really hard
That almost hit Mom's new boyfriend Ray
And yelled, Ho-ho lucky for you she's here
And said that Santa can't stay

Momma said Santa can't stay
Said she told him that twice yesterday
Then a car just like Dad's
Pulled out and drove away
After Mom said Santa couldn't stay

A Long Way Home
1998

%

Same Fool

I'm just the same fool
The old fool
The one fool
That you won't fool no more

'Least not the way that you fooled
The last fool you fooled before

So let the next fool
The new fool
Be a fool
That you will fool for sure

Just know that this fool won't be fooled
Like all those other fools no more

Go find some real fool
No near fool
The kind of fool
That knows what fools are for

That'll give your foolin' heart
Those foolish thrills
It won't stand a chance to ignore

They'll be a fine fool
A flat blind fool
A sort of fool
With not a clue 'bout what's in store

Doing every fool-filled thing you need him to
For however long it is that fools endure

You might be finding
A little lately
That I've been a greatly
Changing man

You don't seem worried
So I'm encouraged
This won't discourage
All your other plans

I'm just the same fool
The old fool
The one fool
That you won't fool no more

Least not the way that you fooled
The last fool you fooled before

No, not the way that you fooled
All those other fools no more

The Curse

Don't you sleep
Don't you have a single moment's peace
Just walk through the darkness
With fears that are deep
And don't you even sleep

Don't you smile
Don't you have happy thoughts for awhile
'Til teardrops and sadness
Both go out of style
No, don't you even smile

These are the things
I wish for you
Deep in my heart
How I hope they come true

And then you'll know
When bad turns to worse
What it's like to live under love's curse

These are the things
I wish for you
Deep in my heart
How I hope they come true

And then you'll know
When bad turns to worse
What it's like to live under love's curse

Don't you try
To have a single
Thought that goes by
Without being haunted
By memories like mine
No, don't you even try

Things Change

She said, Baby things change
I said, But I feel the same
She said, Well let me explain
Baby, how things can change

I said, But that doesn't show
How a love that could grow
Would become so estranged
She said, Well baby things change

She said, Now, now, now,
Baby, don't try
To figure this out
Or ask questions 'bout why
Forever's a promise
No love can survive
And trust with hearts
Just don't apply
She said, 'Cause baby, things change

She said, Now, now, now,
Baby, don't try
To figure this out
Or ask questions 'bout why
Forever's a promise
No love can survive

And trust with hearts
Just don't apply
She said, 'Cause baby things change

Now, now, So baby
I quit tryin'
To figure things out
About all your heart's lyin'
Forever's a promise
We couldn't survive
Hey, I may be slow
But I ain't blind

She said, I still love you so
I said, I don't care to know
She said, You once cried my name
I said, Well baby things change

And let's don't go placing no blame
'Cause you know things can change

Yet to Succeed

Please don't start me cryin'
'Cause I'll go on for days
It don't take a lot
But once this starts, it stays

Talking used to help
Here lately though, that just brings it on

I'll be fine
In time
But right now
I'm just trying to forget you
And clearly I have yet to
Succeed

I think I'll just leave now
Before this hurts too much
Avoiding sights from places
My eyes can't bear to touch

I didn't plan to see you
And then I saw him first

I'll be fine
In time
But right now
I'm just trying to forget you
And clearly I have yet to
Succeed

I'll be fine
In time
But right now
I'm just trying to forget you
And clearly I have yet to
Succeed

I Wouldn't Put It Past Me

I wouldn't put it past me
I wouldn't press my luck
If I were you
I don't believe
I'd take that chance with love

A big chance you'll be taking
The wrong odds is what you're staking us on
And any love you wind up making
Won't pay back half
Of all we've lost

I wouldn't play so boldly
Or push a sure thing too long
'Cause your luck can get thin
Bets not win
Then pretty soon love's up and gone

A big chance you'll be taking
The wrong odds is what you're staking us on
And any love you wind up making
Won't pay back half
Of all we've lost
So I wouldn't put it past me

I wouldn't keep risking heartache
In any more games like these
'Cause there's a way to lose hard
With every card
You'll find out on your knees

A big chance you'll be taking
The wrong odds is what you're staking us on
And any love you wind up making
Won't pay back half
Of all we've lost
So I wouldn't put it past me

I wouldn't put it past me
I wouldn't press my luck
If I were you
I don't believe
I'd take that chance with love

I wouldn't put it past me

These Arms

These arms that hang here by my side
These arms that ache to open wide
Useless arms with nothing left to do
Since these arms stopped holding you

These arms are worthless now to me
They let you go so how good could they be
Just foolish arms
For which I have no need
A pair of arms that grew weak and set love free

Reaching out to embrace
A vacant memory
Finding just the empty space
Around what's left of me

Two arms that failed completely
Arms both scarred so deeply
Keep paying love's costs
With each tragic sway

Trying meekly to assist
My struggle with the truth
Unable to resist
What tears still make us view

Two arms that failed completely
Arms both scarred so deeply
Keep paying love's costs
With each tragic sway

These arms that hang here by my side
These arms that ache to open wide
Useless arms with nothing left to do
Since these arms stopped holding you

Since these arms stopped
Holding you

That's Okay

That's okay
It's alright
No, really everything is cool
This is just
The way I look
When I'm feeling like a fool

Teardrops falling jealous
Drowning in them's just as well as
Drifting on this lonely sea of pain
Could have used another
Night or so to be recovered
Believe the lies I told myself
But just as long as you know

That's okay
It's alright
No, really everything is cool
This is just
The way I look
When I'm feeling like a fool

Voice about us softly mumbling
Words that trip my heart is stumbling
To the ground and crawls there on its knees
I'll embrace small shards of silence
To avoid a loss this violent
And survive love's darkest fears
Just as long as you know

That's okay
It's alright
No, really everything is cool
This is just
The way I look
When I'm feeling like a fool

When I'm feeling like a fool

Only Want You More

Hey girl, hey girl
You warned me to go
But girl, but girl
Little did I know

All the things you told me
About what lay in store
Would only make me want you more

No, not a word
Had one chance to save me
From your love
That wicked love

There's not a prayer
Left for me escaping
From your love
Yeah, that wicked love

Hey girl, hey girl
I begged and hollered please
But girl, but girl
Even from my knees

All the things you told me
About what lay in store
Only made me want you more

No pain can stop
Or rid me what I'm needing
From your love
That wicked love

'Cause what I crave all night
And end each day still seeking
Is your love
Yeah, that wicked love

Hey girl, hey girl
I tried to understand
But girl, but girl
There ain't no way I can

'Cause all the things you told me
About what lay in store
Only made me want you more

Yeah, all those things you told me
About what lay in store
They only made me want you more

I'll Just Take These

I think that I
Will just take a memory
A small one that I know
Real well, then go

What I'll take is all
The happy thoughts I can recall
But I know there won't be much
That I can bear to touch

So I'll just take
What my mind can stand
'Cause there's not a lot
That you can hold
In trembling hands

Just these last few hopeful things
That we left lay
Then quickly leave before
Anymore
Get in my way

So I'll just take
What my mind can stand
'Cause there's not a lot
That you can hold
In trembling hands

Just these last few hopeful things
That we left lay
Then quickly leave before
Anymore
Get in my way

A Long Way Home

Don't look inside
No, don't look there
'Cause you might find
Yourself somewhere

Walkin' 'round
Lost and alone
Without one clue
That it's a long way home

Years and years
Is a lot of time
To drag your heart across
Every rock you find

Hate is deep
And its pull is strong
But the passion's short
Then it's a long way home

I can't take
One single step for you
But I might just help
To find some small pathway through

Don't look back
'Cause you might see
Just how far
All that used to be

Just let your mind
Think on what's gone
And then you'll know
That it's a long way home

Yeah, you'll know
That it's a long way home

You'll find out
That it's a long way home

There ain't no doubt
That it's a long way home

Listen

Listen
In the places you hide
Listen
Through the stillness inside
Listen
To the words that are near
And try to hear

Listen
Take one less step away
Please listen
Love may persuade you to stay
Baby, listen
Past the sound of your fear
And try to hear

Two hearts that doubted now beg to believe
Aching in silence, each whispers a plea
Secrets of longing kept buried away
Sadly they're calling grows weaker each day
Yeah

Please listen
For hope that's been left behind
Listen
To the small traces you find
Baby, please listen
Before this chance disappears
And try to hear

Listen
In the places you hide
Listen
Through the stillness inside
Please, please, baby, listen
For the love that is near
And try to hear

Listen
Take one less step away
Listen
Don't run so far off today
Please, please, baby listen
Push aside all your fears
And try to hear

Listen
Past the sound of all fears
And try to hear

Traveler's Lantern

If deep in the night
You hear a voice calling
Lost and alone
Barely able to speak

With each weary step
Through cold shadows they stumble
Blindly along
Frail, hopeless and weak

Won't you set out a traveler's lantern
Just a small light that they might see
To guide them back home
Before they wander
Into the dark billows
That crash on the sea

At dawn's rise you may find
The footprints of angels
Brought to fellowship there
By your mercy lamp's flame

Walking beside
The weary soul life's forgotten
Bringing comfort and love
And gently leading their way

Won't you set out a traveler's lantern
Just a small light that they might see
To guide them back home
Before they wander
Into the dark billows
That crash on the sea

DISCOGRAPHY

GUITARS, CADILLACS, ETC., ETC. (REPRISE) 1986

It Won't Hurt

I'll Be Gone

South of Cincinnati

Bury Me*

Guitars, Cadillacs*

Twenty Years

Miner's Prayer

©1984 Coal Dust West Music BMI.

* ©1985 Coal Dust West Music BMI.

HILLBILLY DELUXE (REPRISE) 1987

Little Ways

Johnson's Love

Please, Please Baby

Readin,' Rightin,' Rt. 23

1,000 Miles

Throughout All Time

This Drinkin' Will Kill Me

All songs ©1987 Coal Dust West Music BMI.

BUENAS NOCHES FROM A LONELY ROOM (REPRISE) 1988

I Got You

One More Name

What I Don't Know

Buenas Noches From A Lonely Room

I Sang Dixie

Floyd County

Hold On to God

All songs ©1988 Coal Dust West Music BMI.

IF THERE WAS A WAY (REPRISE) 1990

The Distance Between You and Me*

The Heart That You Own*

Takes a Lot to Rock You*

Nothing's Changed Here (co-written with Kostas)†

Sad, Sad Music*

Since I Started Drinkin' Again**

If There Was a Way*

It Only Hurts When I Cry ††

(co-written with Roger Miller)

You're the One†††

Dangerous Man†††

*1990 Coal Dust West Music BMI.
†1990 Coal Dust West Music/Songs of PolyGram International, Inc. BMI.
**1986 Coal Dust West Music BMI.
††1990 Coal Dust West Music/Adam Taylor Music BMI.
†††1979 Coal Dust West Music BMI.

LA CROIX D'AMOUR (REPRISE—RELEASED IN UK ONLY) 1992

Doin' What I Did

THIS TIME (REPRISE) 1993

The Pocket of a Clown

A Thousand Miles from Nowhere

Home for Sale

This Time (co-written with Kostas)*

Two Doors Down (co-written with Kostas)*
King of Fools (co-written with Kostas)*
Fast as You
Try Not to Look So Pretty (co-written with Kostas)*
Wild Ride
Lonesome Roads

GONE (REPRISE) 1995

Sorry You Asked?
Near You
Don't Be Sad
Gone (That'll Be Me)
Nothing (co-written with Kostas)
Never Hold You
This Much I Know
Baby Why Not
One More Night
Heat of Stone (co-written with Kostas)

COME ON CHRISTMAS (REPRISE) 1997

Come On Christmas
Santa Can't Stay

A LONG WAY HOME (REPRISE) 1998

Same Fool
The Curse
Things Change
Yet to Succeed
I Wouldn't Put It Past Me
These Arms
That's Okay
Only Want You More
I'll Just Take These
A Long Way Home
Listen
Traveler's Lantern

All songs ©1998 Coal Dust West Music administered by Warner-Tamerlane Publishing Corp. BMI.